X =

Also by Stephen Berg

Poetry and Prose Poetry

Bearing Weapons
The Queen's Triangle
The Daughters
Nothing in the Word: Versions of Aztec Songs
Clouded Sky by Miklós Radnóti
    (with Steven Polgar and S. J. Marks)
Grief
Oedipus the King (with Diskin Clay)
With Akhmatova at the Black Gates
Sea Ice: Versions of Eskimo Songs
In It
Homage to the Afterlife
Crow with No Mouth: Ikkyū
New and Selected Poems
Sleeping Woman (public art project with the painter Tom Chines,
    along the Schuylkill River in Philadelphia)
The Steel Cricket: Versions 1958–1997
Oblivion
Shaving
Porno Diva Numero Uno
Halo
Footnotes to an Unfinished Poem

Anthologies

Naked Poetry (with Robert Mezey)
Between People (with S. J. Marks and J. Michael Pilz)
About Women (with S. J. Marks)
In Praise of What Persists
Singular Voices
The Body Electric (with David Bonanno and Arthur Vogelsang)
My Business Is Circumference

Poems

by

Stephen

Berg

University of Illinois Press

Urbana and Chicago

X =

∞ This book is printed on acid-free paper.

Library of Congress Cataloging-in-Publication Data
Berg, Stephen.
X = : poems / by Stephen Berg.
p. cm.
ISBN 0-252-02780-9 (cloth : alk. paper)
ISBN 0-252-07091-7 (paper : alk. paper)
I. Title: X equals. II. Title.
PS3552.E7X3   2002
811'.54–dc21   2002000255

I don't know *why* we live. . . . consciousness is an illimitable power, and though at times it may seem all consciousness of misery, yet in the way it propagates itself from wave to wave, so that we never cease to feel, and though at moments we appear to, try to, pray to, there is something that holds one in one's place, makes it a stand-point in the universe which it is probably good not to forsake. You are right in your consciousness that we are all echoes and reverbera-tions of the *same.* . . . Only don't, I beseech you, generalize too much in these sympathies and tendernesses–remember that every life is a special problem which is not yours but another's, and content your-self with the terrible algebra of your own.

    – Henry James, from a letter to Grace Norton, July 28, 1883

Voice

the place bare
only the listener here
stricken
silent in the silence of time's
godless

flow
like wind
sweeping the sacred floor

in the insatiable dream
of love

      – from *Eumenides,* Aeschylus,
        version by Stephen Berg

Acknowledgments

"Thirst," "Death," "Cap," "Speak," "Caritas," "Shitstick," "Thread," "Hooks," and "Windows" previously appeared in *TriQuarterly* 96 (Spring/Summer 1996).

Contents

X =

Biker

he gets on
he gets off he gets on
he rolls it out
he lifts it down the steps
he gets on
he wobbles
he slips his feet into clips
he pushes down
he glides
he steers
he thinks about Zen
he jumps a curb
he pedals uphill onto a new street
he passes the prison
he pedals faster
he adjusts his hands
he sweats a little
he tightens his helmet
he chooses to ride against traffic
he coasts downhill
he pushes faster
he zips past a statue of Hermes cradling a child
he crosses The Drive
he avoids cars
he thinks God Be with Me
he increases his speed up the drive
he twists around joggers
he zips under a stone bridge
he sees the river far out in front of him
he takes the bicycle path
he continues
he goes faster

he pedals nonstop
he hopes to improve
he gives up happiness
he feels his despair even when biking
he ogles a few young girls in shorts skating
he glimpses rowers pulling downriver
he is proud of his legs
he wants the animal language only
he hates the despair of words
he refuses the old music
he seeks a mindless song of this
a declarative ignorance
a blind statement of action
he would explain how the pain of his ignorance and grief translate
    into thigh and calf muscles
he would establish feeling in those locations forever
he is plagued by the concept of intrinsic immortality
he is battered in his chest by Why?
he feels his face in the wind
he once had ideas about awakening to fact
he was much younger then the years the years
he nevertheless pushes hard until his knees hurt
he knows he is almost dead
he remembers his mother's . . . forgets the word
he had a father once
he has arms and legs and thoughts and eyes
he has on gray biking shoes hard pointy tips
he wears a black T-shirt
he cannot express his grief
he can't tell its story
he can't explain the symbol of ! and what it means
the procedure
the ethereal childlike arms

the fear the sobbing throat
he cannot describe the content of the hours
he feels his mouth dismantled by grief
he reaches down rubs his knee
he says all activity is prayer bullshit
he hears Offer it up whatever that means
through the front fork's sensitive nerve
he knows only
road textures each moment
pebbles sticks cracks dirt cement cinders grass

Who

he would never know who gave him his face
he had analyzed the mother the father even nature
he had exhausted the philosophical approaches to identity
he recognized himself of course but who he was seemed to begin
    nowhere end nowhere
he had that now not as idea but as a state of mind
just as on certain spring days you wake
to the perfect temperature and need nothing

Zen

he was sure of it finally
he did not know how
he had always been sure of it
he did not know how
nor could he explain why so tired he still existed that day
why sky leaves tree trunks noises wind continued without a will of
    their own
he was approaching death as he approached love
with the uncontrollable excitement of a child
with the cowardice that always accompanied desire
he accepted each moment
shocked by having a face in the mirror
or torn away from it by the beauty of the world

Thirst

he has never drunk a glass of water when thirsty
he has always done it minutes before he felt the thirst
he must have had an inkling that it was coming
he must have known somehow to stave it off
he has experienced thirst as metaphor: love lust failure fear
he has clung to another's face because of his fear
he has squandered money out of fear
he has professed love due to fear
he has begged for help driven by fear
he has vowed never to hurt himself lashed by fear
he has apologized many times afraid of fear
he has not flown or spoken predicting his fear
he has dreamed himself jailed and cut off in fear
he has confused failure with fear lust with fear love with fear
he has used fear to cut himself off
he will never escape the truth that flesh and blood
    flow out of themselves like water into an unknown mouth
he cannot wait for his thirst so he can be that mouth itself
    unknown to itself mindlessly drinking

Image

he has no desire to call it anything the transparent shape he sees on
the window
he only knows it sticks with him stays with him
he goes back and it is gone
he hopes the nebulous light-created thing is more than a wraith a
trivial illusion
he feels it's identical with prayer or a few stray notes from Billie
Satie Ben
he discovers a need to touch them know them as he knows a
woman's lips their wet live substance
he wants to crush the power of light to disappear or appear at will
he believes it symbolizes the nature of things
he feels it mocks his sense of past and future
the so-called fact of "having time"
he stands in front of the window waiting for the shape
he waits and waits and does see one but the first was the real sign
he has no idea what it looked like now
he knows only its instant of communicated joy
he will read another hundred books ransacking pages
he will underline and scrawl arrows in the margins
he will write exclamation points beside brilliant remarks and drop
them down into the savage clutter of his need sure he is always
ready to be killed
he can't see the killer to kill it first

Mouth

(Warren Rohrer)

he realized his own mouth
he heard the groundlessness of his believing each time he spoke
he realized his own mouth said things all by itself just as the doctor's
    did when it said leukemia
he lived the ordeal by not dwelling on it he said
he was very quiet spoke little heard less
he painted the endless sunset of his mind
he annotated sunsets once a week
he registered the miniscule differences between reds blues greens
he pared his life until it was layers on canvas without the footnotes
    he must have thought of
he realized thus
he painted the unseen landscapes of air
he believed light was the speechless consciousness we seek
as any rose sky blade of grass without a word

Twilight

he sits outside in the dark air
he holds his cold martini
he watches a bird land on a darker branch
he remembers but the memory is only a feeling
he can't see inside his head can't find what it is
he feels it as he feels the twilight inside himself
he is in the still cool realm of light going
he is in the sphere of a curious beauty
he has names for it but doesn't care sipping his drink the bird has
    twitched once or twice but otherwise waits
he enjoys its darkness its nearly invisible shape
he watches the twilight thin to its last phase
he sees the bird disappear without leaving

Death

he grew disgusted with poetry the word the thing
he wanted to be like a Chinese wisdom thinker
he tried to act like a Japanese maniac sword master
he was tired of the bullshit profundities of clear description and
   brilliant thought
he loved gunshops and visited them when he was in the country
   fishing
he'd stand at the counter staring through the glass top at the rows of
   pistols black silver filigreed
he'd ask to hold one aim at a customer a wall
he even bought bullets once a box of bullets
he liked to heft one in his hand taste the tip feel the cold jacket on his
   lips
he remembered when he shot chunks of ice in Iowa
he and Jeff used Jeff's .22 ice on the river splashing up when it was
   hit
he inherited the rifle when Jeff died a few years back
he stored it in the closet took it out leaned it against the wall near his
   desk
he fired it one afternoon at Bill's gun club later left it at Bill's
he looks at his empty hands some days
he doesn't care he doesn't care enough he doesn't care nearly
   enough
beautiful inevitable cosmic law
everyone will die
he looks at his two bare palms strangely his own yet someone else's
he sees them grow light in darkness one night
he has awakened to himself turns the bedroom doorknob with his
   right hand opens the door goes downstairs in darkness holds one
   hand up in front of a window until he can make out each finger
   against the brighter dark of the sky

Mind

he has always heard his mind but not always known what it said

he has heard what seemed like silence or static or broken voices

he has not wanted to hear much of it though now it is all fine

he likes the miserable truths the transient interpretations

he knows the final emptiness behind its churning wheels and violent
    stupidity

he has tried to identify its function its necessity

"that without which Life is impossible air food"

(from Aristotle's section V of the *Metaphysics*)

he has even forced himself for days to work on problems like eternity
    immortality faith salvation terms the mind sends up like gaudy
    rockets to distract us

he has wanted to smash himself against those words like a brick
    hurled through a window

he has spoiled ordinary days

he has haunted their vicinity like a starved dog

he has crippled himself with oneness and being

he has tried to mask his ignorance like that

he still cannot rest in the physical world like a rat or a bird or a
    simple flower but memorized without trying Blake's poem about
    killing a fly that ends "Then am I / A happy fly / If I live / Or if I
    die" and still can't make his life

Death

he saw her after the operation
he stood over her in ICU
he spoke and tried to reach her
he touched her hand
he held it rubbed it said
he heard the mumbled fragments
he heard the blip of the monitor
he was waiting for her to wake
he wanted her to wake to prove she would live
he smoothed the sheets poured water
he rearranged the flowers
he imagined her face lost forever
he could hear her breath regular breaths
he was listening he stood there at least an hour
he watched her relaxed face which did not change
he observed her expression placid blank
he asked the nurse how she was doing
he felt something like love for the human world a pang
he would include himself in that and everyone he knew
he bent over and kissed her brow
he would never know the fruit of their love
he had been taught the lesson of grief for no one in particular

Food

he boils red bliss potatoes
he drains them holds them under cold water
he takes out the big knife
cuts them into chunks
chops celery Vidalia onion parsley
mixes it all grinds in pepper
he pours a few dashes of olive oil into balsamic vinegar
squeezes lemon adds pepper tastes it
he stirs it with a fork
he dribbles it onto the salad tastes it
he loves the fresh clear taste of it
he rips off a square of waxed paper places it on top of the bowl
he slips it into the fridge to cool
he has been thinking of her arms and cold lips
he has seen her eyes grow tender again
he can easily call up her light blonde hair it comes back by itself
    thighs inner darknesses silences of not being able to say it
he was putting down the bowl on a cold shelf
he was noticing the frosty metal edge
he finds a clear place for the bowl
he shuts the door with unusual care
her small being for years as close as his
her animal look just emerging from grass at dawn
he sees it whatever he does like the shining sharp steel blade

Cap

he put on the cap because he wanted to cover his head
he wanted the cotton fishing cap on
he liked the pale green and gray the three holes on each side
he needed the feeling of a cap
he took it off and rolled the peak
he wanted to shade his eyes
he could see the peak just above his eyes a shadow like someone's
    disembodied hand
he thought that hand might help
he prayed to his books scattered like trash at his feet
he spoke to the torn paper at his feet
he stared at the walled-up fireplace
he imagined a fire there pathetic flames
he would never give in to the wish that made him heavy
he heard the word *soul* tear him in two like thick dry paper
his curse everyone's a history with only one word to justify existence
    not really
he assumed fate was at the root of even wearing his cap
he tilted it slightly to the left
he thought of the word *sky* Groddek's word in his essay "Language"
    on "inner muteness"
he opened the refrigerator drank juice
he walked outside where the accidental sun embraced his head

Impotence

he woke to it
he had no choice
he was flayed in the dream
he walked to the bathroom
he washed brushed looked at himself
he recognized himself
he dropped the towel
he did not pick it up
he put on a dirty shirt clean underpants old pants sneakers combed
    his hair
he looked around the kitchen for coffee
he heard TV somewhere outside
he heard shards of voices
he had no choice knowing the world
he of course was trying to understand but had never been given that
    gift by others and so failed himself
his problem of what to do his question of self
his this or that here or there
he would struggle again as always with the thing words had never
    been able to touch not true
he had been touched by words healed even but now
he was torn by beliefs unknown to him
he hated the music that once consoled
he could not bear it
he heard the blank bleak stupidity in his head like a fist on a tabletop
he looked at the ravishing birch out back
he saw how its leaves moved and stayed quiet as a god

Listener

he heard the phone
he picked up the receiver
he said hello
he took off his glasses
he moved a letter on his desk
he heard her say and not say
he asked he asked again
he knew her words weren't the real words
he joked
he had that old wish for God a signpost
he needed it but it was all weakness
he even heard a biblical sigh wisdom icons
he could feel the storm of pain approaching
he asked anyhow
he heard the other one's grieving facts
he could do nothing except talk
he advised he soothed he did all that
he listened
he heard every syllable there was
he thought troops were marching upstairs in a house in a fallen
    country
he heard birds at the same time
he understood there could be birds and desolation
he knew this was a lesson he resisted always
he blessed the victims of bad luck
he blessed the victims of good luck
he wanted to tear out someone's eyes someone who deserved all that
    happens

Earth

in the taxi going downtown
he heard the black driver say "'Agree with the earth' that's what my
    father told me
that's what city people don't know"

Death

he knew always returning it would revise his longing
he knew it would force desire to attack desire
he knew it would make him kneel invisibly inside
he knew it would ask and ask until he bled answers
he knew he would never face it until it came
he knew all the theories would be worn out by its transparent gaze
he knew the anonymous third person would not save him
he knew beauty was a mere delay a passion of attentive order
he knew to distract himself work play
he knew words were tiny stones that punctured a paper screen
he knew others suffered this same eon of lost joy
he knew no one's skill or strength could stop it
he knew the silent glorious *No* behind it all
he knew the simultaneous misery of *Yes*
he was all he could be
he knew even so that the tiniest ant or grain of dirt contained a
     hopeless fortune
he knew the problem of change would be solved
he knew a different life so possible hung just out of reach
he felt the truth the crime whose punishment was the simple
     undeniable fact of one's life as it is
he wanted to scour all the forms of knowing all the cases all the
     distinctions theories self-deceptive suicidal turns of mind of
     action of meditated willed attitude until the process yielded
     freedom
he knew the fraud of serious words
he knew the crippling fact that happiness and death were twins in
     his case as the Greeks foretold
he saw the blinding gift how each of us is absent how we struggle to
     experience to realize it right now but can't and therefore what
     we do is look at things and talk and eat and touch

Death

he wrote it in the upper left-hand corner of the blank page

he wanted to list every word that occurred under that heading

he thought a kind of trance would reveal a meaning a redemption

he wanted to believe in a system at least for a few minutes a simple
act of magic a way out of the torment of disappearance

he saw the word death as a black wall infinitely thick black is what
you entered once you broke through that wall

he knew for now he lived on this side of it where the light is

he was still committed to the side of light and movement

he could feel all the people he knew who had died like a permanent
silence not like a bell's last note because the bell remained and
could be struck again

he heard that silence like someone without a tongue under torture
without a throat

he would sit for hours concentrating on this

he slept and it tinged even sexual dreams

he practiced for the day when it would happen by erasing himself by
never using the word *I* by pounding his face with an imaginary
hammer ears eyes nose mouth eradicated so he'd be ready

Dream

he dreamed and dreamed and dreamed and dreamed and dreamed
he dreamed her sitting in a chair like a queen watching him
he saw her look at him hard
he heard "Jerry Robbins wore my blouse then hung it on a hook in
    the closet ruined it there's a dent in the cloth where the hook
    was"
he could feel in the dream the climate of her hatred
he knew from being in the dream with her that his life was saturated
    by the menace and judgment of her stare
he breathed it as he breathed the air
he begged himself for the grace the word grace promised
he had been "sadly amputated" one called it
he wanted to grip his mind like the handle of a hammer and fix it by
    using it to fix itself
he knew how not being able to might in fact be grace

Speak

he knew these notes did nothing helped no one nevertheless
he wanted back into the non-metaphysical realm of hard fact of
    accepted concrete temporary fact and how to be there how to let
    grace generate trust
physical physical cried the brass hinges on his two front doors
physical wept the ceilings and walls
physical pleaded the nails on his own two hands
physical prayed the green shrubs rocks trees in his yard
physical bled his own inner heart battered by love
physical hoped his eyes because they saw without trying
physical whispered his mouth grateful for its breath its noises
physical groaned his aching left knee with its clicking tendon
physical strode the sky permanently locked up there above like a
    bank safe door
physical horizon gnawed at the sky with its buildings hills valleys
    distances
physical called out to God last dissonant chords of hope in the belly
    and larynx
physical some nights that seemed to cry by themselves because
    Mankind's sorrow like the permanent sky is
physical the delicate ant tiptoeing across my patio
physical its mate the free fly diving crawling zigzagging free
physical the nose's discriminatory gifts symbolic shape ability to put
    itself almost anywhere yes even there there in its need to do
    more than simply smell
physical your absence from me at this very time reading these crude
    words
physical your desire and mine to connect through the voice that
    reaches into the space where you could be
physical your waking and your death all alone without me me
    without you
physical our ashes miles apart at first destined to meet
physical your calm ordinary morning drinking a first coffee

physical the unexpected release from torment

physical the boiled milk you whip to a froth and pour atop your
    coffee

physical the slice of rye that jumps hot from the toaster

physical the term "Being" which has several senses

physical the "Why we should seek for other entities apart from
    sensible things and the Intermediates"

physical "That which does not exist may come to be, but nothing
    which cannot exist comes to be"

physical such wild ideas sprung from passionate minds that can't
    stop themselves from delving forgive them forgive their stream
    of words of words seeking words

physical Rimbaud's little-known "twin assholes"

physical the hole in the ground where I shall be put

physical my fear of disappearance and attempts to build a mind that
    can stand it

physical dead friends parents "which once gained increase through
    something else by contact"

physical the growing silence around each person thing thought
    silence itself becoming the agent of a first cause

physical the unfelt feeling buried in every word

physical the shed feather I came across in a huge field in Vermont its
    four brown streaks its white ground its communicated hint of a
    meaning I still can't formulate

physical the ordained miracle of standing sitting lying down

physical the hand-finished stainless steel sink

physical the text of words that hang between the physical and the
    musical or to say it differently between the world of tactile fact
    and the world of auditory time

physical the images inside my head of a face

physical the idea that the physical masks another perhaps physical
    reality but not physical like this one

physical the squirrel's hyper-acute awareness its muscles its flights
     its tenacious swift thefts and escapes
physical the grateful heavy eyelids at night the sleep
physical "The grandest efforts of poetry are where the imagination is
     called forth, not to produce a distinct form, but a strong working
     of the mind, still offering what is still repelled, and again
     creating what is again rejected; the result being what the poet
     wishes to impress, namely, the substitution of a sublime feeling
     of the unimaginable for a mere image"
physical my love of that sentence my inability to fully comprehend it
     my belief in it my homage
physical my hand that traverses the soft wet gash from behind and
     continues
physical that pup whose leap from a daughter's lap into the street put
     it under a wheel smashed it
physical the denigrated abstractions that ride herd over men
physical the wish of indisputable immortality
physical the fingertip that selects keys
physical the insatiable desire to generalize
physical Bill's theory of inadequacy whenever he talks about himself
physical Michael's love of God through surrender is all that's left
physical the chanted breath behind whose systematic tongue lurks a
     final meaning a revelation that will solve everything and make
     us happy and release us from the physical
physical Melville's obsession his decision to use the harpoon his soul
     curled against a wall his hanging saint
Physical Tolstoi's "Death is no more" after the petty official's diseased
     body forces him into the metaphysical-physical
physical Wittgenstein's "Even if his dream were actually connected
     with the noise of the rain" his love of "I believe" his hatred of "I
     know" his physical prostate cancer
physical Chekhov's disregarded TB surgical kindness trip across icy
     wilderness to reform a prison cure his depression

physical Bellow's death-lion befriending death Henderson's hand on
the lion's flank
physical Ikkyū's pure lack of identity like wind sweeping in
dissolving into a neutral presence of air
physical Toshiko's hands glazing clay for the fire
physical the untold weeping behind this that I can't express whereas
Larkin does so poignantly everywhere "There is an evening
coming in / Across the fields, one never seen before, / That lights
no lamps." etc.
physical the most physical word is *etc.* why I can't say
physical Frost's rhythmical textures his lines have surfaces like
leaves and stones
physical the music of all the failed poetry right under my hands no
but because I gave it up to the form I can't complain
physical all theories like this one that cannot end their attempts to
prove themselves right
physical the talks in therapy that seem to help to lead me through the
valley
physical the brain tumors of three friends
physical Ozalea's skinny black body cleaning mildew off the tub
physical the form that commits you to it or causes resistance to
seduce you into its imperfect unresolvable trust so you can speak
at all even though ridiculously
physical my problem that maybe the physical is more than the
physical
physical the words that hurt because of how they scar mind heart
ability to trust love
physical darkness which never fails to come at the end
physical amazement the need for meaning
physical Proust's use of individuals through whom we suffer to draw
nearer to the divine form to divinities
physical my disgust at not being able to be other than myself
physical simplicity that does not give up enough

physical the sainthood of attention whatever one's mood

physical any rule that helps one to go on

physical the breaking of the rule when it fails

physical "Lord Jesus Christ, have mercy on me" because Franny
believed it so completely her lips spoke silently without having to
try the prayer

physical the dream of my dentist who says of course I'll save your
teeth putting his groceries down on a car hood while some
homeless bum comes up and demands money and the green
vegetables and grains spill from the bag onto red metal

physical someone uttered in my sleep trying to help me take death in
like a kiss awakening's when you *are* the third person singular
breathing in the flesh myth symbol

physical us who evaporate and become indecipherable *you* and *I* did
you see that plump truculent blue jay perched a second ago on a
garden chair leave us?

Caritas

he had a map in his mind where each one sat on a crate or squatted
stood stretched out his or her hand holding a paper cup on
Walnut Chestnut 17th 18th 16th everywhere downtown
demanding money for food

he alternated between resentment anger and practicing compassion
for those who had so little compared to him imagined himself
rich giving them thousands in fact all he did was drop dimes and
quarters sometimes nothing in their cups

he saw a millionaire friend of his once bend with great gentleness
over one swaddled in a filthy blanket say quiet words then take
out a large bill and hand it over

he had constructed a technique for not experiencing how low they
were for repressing his fear of being them swathed in grime and
rags companioned by their wounded plastic garbage bags
swollen with all they owned he could walk by without a twinge
of guilt for not kneeling to sympathize to kiss

he had eliminated his original persistent fantasy of taking one home
especially the old man trembling on Locust Street so bent he
couldn't look up to thank you when he thanked you letting him
sleep in a room of his huge house like family maybe having him
clean fix things bringing him meals

he hadn't done it and never would the basic dog-eat-dog that's-*his*-
problem primitive survival mode was what impelled him purged
this illusion of true purpose

he absorbed their poverty the way body absorbs and filters out air
polluted by car exhaust factories whatever shit falls out from
industry

he knew some helpless part of his soul needed them there to
reinforce his illusion of success needed his resignation his
acceptance of their fate it seemed to solve the incessant inner
struggle of accepting his own death really letting it be at last
until you feel your heart's a purely loving organ

he killed in his mind the duplicate of himself listening to the moron
     sprawled drooling half-speechless listened so well the man was
     "cured" but of what? the misfortune of our differences? the
     intrinsic tragedy of class?
he was amazed they had appeared at all first naturally familiar
     expected like weeds clouds puffs of wind increasing in
     importance until the days would be decimated less than real
     some mystic sacred meaning erased if each morning they did not
     dot the sidewalks

Cure

he took his mother's clock to the store where they fixed old clocks
he told the watchmaker to find a missing minute hand that would
    match the thin blue steel one that was left
he tilted the clock sideways to inspect the porcelain face's elegant
    wavy surface like fresh milk in sunlight
he said he wanted it fixed only if the new parts were original
he concentrated on the clock because of a dying love or a
    misunderstanding based on a wrong choice of terms
he recognized the constant struggle in himself to find terms that
    explained feelings bring in history cure
he wanted to connect his mother to all the women he knew
he was trying to analyze his state of current grief
he remembered when she would hate him her violent words ticking
    inside him like time inside the antique machinery
he knew his mind had narrowed itself to the single aim of cure to
    cure himself of what?
he picked up the clock repaired perfectly cleaned oiled the brass case
    polished
he wound it with a key every eight days but rarely looked at it
he would walk past it hear its delicate tick
he would admire its oblong beauty
he would invest the meaning of the word cure in this object cure of
    needing women of cure of disappointment
he would cure himself by loving the object by knowing each nick
    and tiny scratch
he would reduce his voice to the loudness of the clock so he would
    not be heard unless you got very close to him but you would
    hardly see him anyway by then he would have grown
    transparent like the beveled glass case of the clock his face as
    white as the milky enamel face oh words "the dissonance
    between the means and their use" a permanent wound so deep it
    feels like exposed bone

Compulsion

he heard bloodcells the single blur of a word referring to
he knew bloodcells as a word referring to his body to
he had never seen blood cells except in a science magazine or
he had seen his own blood run from a cut and
he heard the doctor say bloodcells in urine or
he was surely doomed by the word bloodcells the panic the
he had always been poor at patience poor at logic at
he had a mind that condemned him instantly to
he saw the specialist who took blood for a slide and
he would see the urologist on Monday but
he lay down on the table pants off and
he saw them raise a shield a sheet at his navel to blind him to
he felt the tube slide slowly into his penis up it but
he knew the nausea of how wrong it was to
he had made out a will that weekend leaving everything to his
    beloved wife the nothing of a small insurance policy a few books
    papers worthless objects he had nothing to leave except his
    daughters whatever they found on the white table he heard "a
    slight irritation" got up and put his pants on
he dreamt that night he and Jack Nicholson lay naked on a chaise
    drinking champagne by Nicholson's pool in Hollywood young
    women in bikinis strolled stopped to talk they were naked too the
    blue shimmer of the water beside him the glasses on the glass
    table sky power the long relaxed penis of his movie buddy all the
    resolution he did not know he had been yearning for in a life so
    viciously incomplete

Dog

he wanted to return as a dog that hot July day sitting with her on the
couch dogs have no consciousness of lust or shame their snouts
avid for smell

he wanted to slip off the couch down on his knees and kiss her
thighs thin cotton dress shadow of crotch

he was having this image in the present forty-five years later his
insoluble life with women his consciousness a thing he prayed
for disaster hummed at the edges of the real for him the ominous
the numinous intolerable gift of abuse perception continued but
could be interrupted by disaster any time suicide seemed in
some form reasonable

he wanted to be a dog that day because it could not think it would
give itself over to her flesh enslave itself haunt its owner by
pleading with its eyes the way dogs do once they've been fed you
can even wallow your face in its coat hold its little head in your
hands kiss it feel consoled

he was in the present but did not want to be because here
consciousness is this is who he is his mind not what he wants it
to be the wrong mind insoluble for too long he would have torn it
out like a dead bush but it continued its torment turned women
into objects of dread and need of transferential terror these
preliminaries kept beating at him like wasps inside their papery
cage fused with life he couldn't pin down then and now with a
story

he had no idea he'd dream he'd knock on her door one evening hear
     her call "Come in" open the bathroom door see her in the tub
     breasts glistening with soap and water calm she looked at him
     standing there in the doorway chatted briefly until he closed the
     door scared didn't even walk in and kiss her wet nipples later
     when she was dressed they roll around on her bed like kids
     another instance of the same an entire story would not solve it
     would merely be poetic admirable perhaps entertaining
     redeeming enviable a technical feat without wisdom unless he
     found terms that could help him change relive it
he knew the roots were so deep only death would resolve it
he knew it had happened to him before he knew who he was
he knew it had taken him this long to wake at all because waking
     equaled death
he knew each of these rungs led somewhere or nowhere
he knew his executioner had been executed herself had no choice
he knew he was really still alive
he had doubted he was alive doubt so intense he had to look in the
     mirror hundreds of times each day
he still needs to make lists to understand to hold on
he likes to imagine these lists are rungs leading to the face of God
he has good days when desire and time agree
he analyzes religious terms and abandons them again and again
he had many dogs as a child and still wants to come back as one
he still can't name what he needs that he never got
he loves the fact that a dog is smaller than he is walks on a leash can
     learn obeys licks his face and hands
he still assumes the darkness teems with hating eyes
he trusts if he collects enough facts in the right order release from
     this will occur
he sees a dog as the self he'll never be so deeply taken care of by the
     universe by life itself that the speech of his maimed mind will
     never touch this beast of easy unenlightened love

Shitstick

he had read so much Zen it was coming out of his ears did nothing
    ruined his common sense confused irritated infuriated
he knew he had gone to it because of pain bought all the books
    underlined arrowed starred bracketed memorized forgot picked
    out passages that struck a chord flotsam and jetsam of salvation
he knew he was trying to ward off life the whole enlightenment
    shtick sucked him in he sat half-closed his eyes let thoughts float
    in out across down up
he even believed for very brief moments that it had happened he was
    there he knew what he knew in a deep deep way but then
    immediately he would be who he was again the same old stupid
    ordinary Steve
he for years probably read every day something from those texts
    usually early each morning first thing before coffee or while he
    made it what an asshole he thought what great stuff he thought
    what insanity fun trash epitome of wisdom
he wanted to fathom his place in the universe especially given death
    yes of course the great amazing pain in the ass death the sexual
    thrill the time-eater death the word of words the horrible
    mommy-maw of no more me
he read one day that if anything bothered you all you had to do was
    invoke the phrase "a dried shitstick" hold it in your mind one of
    many instructions koans cuckoo ideas embedded in the tradition
he forgot it he bumped into it now and then until one day he found
    himself repeating the phrase automatically God! until hard to
    believe he actually had the phrase like one of those gold-lettered
    signs on real estate office windows MIDTOWN REALTY fixed
    between him and the world "a dried shitstick" right there
    whatever he saw touched kissed pondered ate

Eliot

he imagined himself as an infant in a pair of anonymous hands to
    him at that age anonymous but most personal his mother's
    tending hands cradling him bathing him his lips and eyes
    beginning
he tried to connect his life at sixty-eight to this tiny helpless being
    without intellect yet sheer flesh not even mind yet
he could only do this by assessing his true state in the present
    marriage friends work money religious core intestinal condition
    mood was he Eliot?
he could only reinstate the truth of that time by recreating himself
    then how sweetly held how cleaned how dried and soothed and
    bedded how responded to when the cells wept or skull wailed or
    belly ruthlessly appealed poor pure body before identity could he
    be Eliot?
he would scrutinize dreams for the truth but they gave him too much
    to interpret his understanding reeled from their rich intricate
    infinities their dearth of overt intellect it was intellect that
    seemed to hide itself under life as a late flower in a bitter season
    intellect the blue lily on a gangly stem like Eliot
he saw its miracle of mind its unforced blend of terror pity thought a
    kind of soul *eidolon* is that the soul? vapor with a tiny batlike cry
    spinning into the earth the double of what we see when we stand
    in front of anyone of ourselves in the mirror hair color shape of
    eye nose lips the exact physical duplicate of the physical but no
    more solid than the weather *eidolon* Eliot's quest

he wanted to be able to hold the mind like a knife or hammer use it
to fix things but it was always out of reach always right here
intellect or even ego or the world itself like *phobos* who strangles
the breath out of a man freezes him to the spot like dry ice to the
skin mood of Eliot he had a dream of himself finally in which
Eliot supplies himself with a photograph of Eliot for an
international exhibition of poetry at first he suggests other texts
but a disembodied voice commands "Supply Eliot" and Eliot has
to supply shots of himself leaning back on the railing of a cruise
ship on its way to Cuba and one of him and his cousin at Cape
Anne Eliot wears a black cowboy hat his arm around her as if
intellect really doesn't matter when circumstances permit but he
had a broken soul that would not stop howling refining fire
trying to express what the fires told him the vedic fires the
chanted excremental non-transcendences of the *Upanishads*
dizzying eastern texts where Time and Matter merge into one
great flame that lets us be here his silent eyes his nervous
breakdown eyes peering at us through pained caring music

Humiliation

he knew his own white mind hated them spontaneously like genetic
    code deciding the fate of a heart
he knew pity and the burden of its slowly accumulated weight a
    consciousness of yearning futile prayers
he saw black everywhere cigar-colored men and women
he could foresee his death in them his failure to rise above their
    black poor lives their drawls his vulnerable laws
justice he wanted justice to eliminate poverty cure his mind of the
    innate mechanisms that erupted converted his identity into
    someone else who stood for things he didn't believe in as if
    blackness caused a second identity to occur like a shield inside
    against compassion
he'd catch himself cursing the differences the facts cut to a movie
    starring Sidney Poitier on TV he has to pee fleeing from South
    African police you white foreskin must unzip fly lift out his penis
    because his hands are numb from torture from having his balls
    electrocuted in jail on TV we see them country by country shot
    starved beaten hung on blackness is the title of the play on being
    white not black Poitier had been in prison for ten years he
    realized that the image of himself was more real than he was
    think of the mirror you wash your face in each day I mean its
    true purpose is it to avoid humiliation should it be to rehearse
    humiliation by concentrating on the image of your face so hard
    so long that the you outside the mirror staring disappears to you
    and all you are is the image in the glass no longer searching for
    yourself
O soul O much more destitute than the soul

Phonefun

O death death death kept battering at his head until he was nearly
    crazy with it the fact the inevitable event he'd be the center of the
    star attended lamented for diagnosed consoled all the
    unbearable good-byes
he could only think of calling her death's duplicate to talk to see
    where talk went when it got this way when he saw himself gone
    forever do it by phone forget death
he had seen others go suddenly slowly painlessly in agony heart
    failure cancer suicide
he had imagined every death for himself even as a heroic spy
    captured by a bad country tortured for secrets he would not tell
    testicles burned fingernails torn out eyeballs pierced until the
    camera close-ups his face his iron refusal to confess as he dies
    for his idiot country
he had set himself up as a brain surgeon who collapses while
    operating on Reagan's tumor and fortunately Reagan dies on the
    table
he had conjured himself as a researcher infected with bacteria from
    a shattered vial
O death Homeric reason for song especially if the hero's young what
    opportunities are left in our age to die a hero
I could give away every cent table chair shirt car and live on the
    street but would that be heroic I could slash my wrists in
    homage to Rwandan suffering I could dress up like Simone Weil
    plain homely disgustingly cheap and starve myself to death
    because of whatever injustice why shouldn't I beg why shouldn't
    I starve why shouldn't I give my pay to others

I'd rather get my cock sucked on the phone by a high school
     girlfriend who always loved to do it that way talking a blue
     streak I could call her any time after awhile she'd begin crooning
     whispering words like delicious O hard long thing O give it to
     me ease it deep into my mouth come on my face I want to lick
     the head bite the rim a little suck on the tip until you come just
     hold its stone-hard length against my cheek so I can gobble it
     take it all the way in until you explode at the back of my throat
     sweet cock sweet baby O thick hard baby bursting with cum
God's voice like a wall between me and death

Dream

he asked whose poem is it yours or mine it's yours now look at those
    lines those images listen to that music
he was shown panoramic views of Africa huge color shots of blacks
    milling across plains landscapes of sand and rock something
    very valuable was at stake but secret in the dream unknowable
    palpable invisible beautiful a mood ominous poisonous
he heard words combining in a strange purgatorial song hopeful
    troubling threnody of loss
self could never be known unless he listened
world could never be known unless he heard
friends could never be known unless he learned the melody
life could never be lived unless he could hum it
death could never be faced unless he stripped silence from it
it was nobody's poem he realized hearing it crumble in his ear
it was a residue of some accidental clash among leaves or stars the
    echo of an echo no one could hear
he slipped into bed that night early not to sleep but to listen for what
    he thought might come if he simply lay there and waited through
    the whole night
he recalled that the man in the dream holding the photographs was
    like a god offering images of a new life merely step into the
    landscape enter one of the silent empires dominated by no
    known king

Poetry

Wordsworth's *Immortality Ode* Donne's *Elegy X* Larkin's *Church
    Going* Whitman's cradle Dickinson's Split the lark and you'll
    hear the music & I fish until the sky turns blue / Weary of self-
    torture Lowell's resisted humility Berryman's flayed phrases all
    the poignant voices healing they do heal he believed but how
he tried to find out what it meant mainly to others I guess but surely
    to himself writing himself lines stanzas paragraphs
    misunderstandings of form attempts at form failures at form
    thoughts about form in the meditative mind that accompanies
    every act word meaning
he faced his idea that he had never learned how to write had never
    understood what it was for
he began to dream another language a dream of English that
    corresponded to the trees to the abiding presence of his body
    strong fragile integer of unnecessary disrupted *ars poetica* year
    2002 bearing down on him like a Mack truck
say death is three weeks away could you say why you write? could
    he? say sitting on the stool above your computer you had to
    justify the least peep out of your mouth
he heard himself like the final stanza of a good poem about hell
    which would describe in concrete detail both the Homeric
    ripped-open thigh and black death cloud and the sorrow of his
    face gravity pulling at it what he remembered was joy was when
    he masturbated a friend "phonefun" is what they called it five
    times at least she could do herself talking listening to him talk
    her through five orgasms the day before they had analyzed WW's
    Ode on the phone argued what "thoughts that do lie too deep for
    tears" really means he drew his finger along her wet pussy in his
    mind it was everything when he did it he had to live without it
    he laughed at it he loved Groucho's answer to "What would you
    do if you could live your life again?" "Try more positions."

Wall

he had to find out what freedom is not Sartre's "useless passion" not
    Augustine's infinite ladder to the face of God not Wittgenstein's
    silence not Dickinson's Quite empty quite at rest but the sense
    that anywhere is where he is anytime when
he felt its imperative cry some nameless bird in his chest Afflicts me
    as a setting sun sang Dickinson
he could call up a hundred lines phrases to describe it the lack of it
    the staring at a wall the wall itself the blank impassive nothing
    "You can't" Van Gogh would hear standing in front of a canvas
    unable to paint
he would sit at the wall and examine its white granular skin
he would lean against it to cool his cheek
he'd run his right hand slowly along its face like a slug
he'd curse its dumb indifference
he even one day pushed his head as hard as he could against it held
    it there almost an hour until the spot on his skull ached
he sat cross-legged on the floor at home in front of it until he felt
    another's fist like a sphere of heat inside him grinding his ribs to
    pieces
he would hear *free me free me* chirp in his throat and still hears it his
    pores nails hair eyelashes knees
he sees it now in the transparent featureless face whose unseen lips
    open like the vast world-wall Oedipus stabbed out of his own
    head but don't speak
he hears a woman in the night utter "Love . . ."
he hears his mother's "I think not . . ."

Object

he had objects had the imagination of objects inside his parents' first
  Plymouth convertible 1951 four-door cream dash plastic fins its
  pungent vinyl seats and wheel was one
he even envied its perfection swollen metal fenders hood sloped
  trunk sleek chrome door handles trim bumpers its Powerglide its
  ornament shaped like a miniature silver galleon
he would go down to the apartment garage and sit in it alone and
  clutch the wheel with both hands and imitate steering it work
  the pedals peer through the windshield in his mind see roads
  trees hills and rivers
he had objects the fielder's mitt he oiled daily and punched a pocket
  into
he had objects the gut-strung tennis racket the can of balls white
  sneakers shorts
he had objects the Graflex D he could capture things in 1/1000th of a
  second focal plane shutter single lens reflex
he had fighter planes built out of balsa and glue bird bones stones
  feathers twigs shaped like ideas
he had an array of baseball cards that still smelled like bubble gum
  his father's dirty poker deck rubbers old keys
he had a cigar box crammed with all kinds of shit from coins to
  stamps to postcards newspaper shots of war a swimming medal
  pliers 8th Army insignia shaped like a shield crossed by a golden
  sword of lightning
he had a photo of a girl whose face he still remembers exactly as it
  was radiantly poisoned with unconsciousness plus notes from
  her a coil of hair
he had different leaves associated with people's faces why he wasn't
  sure he just thought that way maybe sixty barely able to be held
  lest they dissolve in his hand those in a separate cardboard box
he had dimes because of their smooth small feel he loved to click his
  fingernail along their ribbed edges rub the female face

he had two penknives one that snapped open with a button one you
    had to pull out yourself curved happy blades
he had a one dollar bill someone had written on in red pen: "watch
    this fly"
he had magazines of women stripped doing things to themselves
    stared at to get hard
he had stacks of blank paper for the sake of their clarity
he can't remember all of it the things that proved he had a place in
    this world nor the voice he did not have to explain his crazy
    family where a woman squeezed him in her fist like a black
    diamond

Satori,
the Immediate Presence Of *(1954, NYC)*

he dreamt he was crossing Broadway at 10th and she appeared in
    the middle of the street crossing also diagonally cars at a red
    light throbbing

he looked up saw her face again after the years she smiled blurted
    "How are you?" in that automatic common way one does
    surprised before thinking seeing someone who meant who
    means what?

he passed her refused to look back looked back her long brown legs
    in shorts turning the corner she was gone again gone

he had pushed her far down in his mind under the flow of daily
    detail a word merely in memory now but he always knew she
    was still there inside the way she was when they loved

he knew this again when he saw her and didn't stop of course they
    were in the middle of the street in a lull of traffic but he could
    have turned and gone with her and talked

he could have asked how she was did she still feel the same

he knew he felt the same or could or would rapidly again in her
    presence

he had been held by her with a kindness he had never known

he had wept simply because of who she was

he had heard her say I love you because of what you are

he had been unable to understand her as deeply freely as she
    understood him

he was unable to give himself to her though he loved her until one
    day she turned away from him

he was told this in a cheap restaurant and wept in front of the
    customers while she led him out by his arm that's when time
    changed into the hell of time because he could not have her his
    unconscious possession of her had been violated severed he was
    living in the first phase of that lesson

he thought years later the whole thing had been a secret he hadn't
   realized he was keeping from himself and the secret was his
   actual self the self that needed something from a woman so
   painfully it was too devastating to face until she broke off with
   him and he was forced to face it whatever it was he was living it
   in time's hell whatever it was and still is he could not get rid of it
   ameliorate himself so his desire and unredeemable loss
   somehow would be cured fused into a new spirit
he could not have her but he could not stop needing her so time
   became a hellish condition one lived through like disease like a
   haze that blocked the present from one's senses all that mattered
   was this woman this inaccessible figure of salvation who
   rejected him would never return be his
he would have to walk through this for years working on it allowing
   it to work on him and he did and it did
he never was sure what it meant except in psychological terms fear
   of being left fear of being alone pool of guilt from an earlier life
   mother's ambivalence and so on and so on until the cry in his
   own ears of himself trying to grasp what had happened made
   him sick suicidally sick those were some general terms
he lived his life and didn't want to find specific terms to explain this
   to himself or to others just enough to sketch it out so you could
   put it together imagine it until two years after she left he visited a
   Zen teacher and told him about this pain he had been plunged
   into and heard the man say "She's your koan" quenched white
   hot iron need O isn't need at the root of it like his dream of a
   glowing penis gorgeous burnished irresistible a great
   archaeological find in a musuem display case he felt like two
   people like a shadow of himself the outline of a second person a
   voice not quite really here always drifting into the dread of
   anticipation but moments when he could accept what his senses
   gave him without an object occurred wisps of gratitude

he did not know how deeply ingrained unconscious expectations are

he said to himself remember when you would lay together and feel
    peacefully happy for the first time remember how she accepted
    you how palpable sanction was like a glass of good red wine or
    the warmth of an actual hand but what would it be like without
    her without an object

he was rambling because he knew nothing about this but theory
    what Benoit pictures as a man in a room windows barred door
    open the man stands at the window clutching the bars fascinated
    by the outside world his keenness for the images outside making
    his two hands violently contract he can't let go of the bars
    nothing shuts him in but the crispation of his own hands
    rambling quoting seeking incapable of pure attention

he could not turn those images into a story's knowing

he was so deep in the past now everything was memory memory of a
    memory expectation

he was so deep in confusion all he could expect was pain

he knew his random bitternesses sprung from this

he was so fearful of losing what he had getting what he wanted he
    lived half-paralyzed like a point without dimension or situation
    perhaps without time perhaps these words like bars on a
    window in his way perhaps he would never know what his
    doubt was

he believed writing would accomplish it he believed writing it
    wouldn't be worth shit her smile her mind in his mind his mind
    in hers "How are you?"

he realized he hadn't answered as they passed because of how
    quickly it happened? because to her he would have answered
    honestly and wept this raw exploration always active in him his
    lone flesh permeated with her now a witless desolated ghost
    pacing his mind

he wakes today this crude speech in his mind poor way to bow to a
nameless audience and hears "How are you?" back there in the
asphalt middle of Broadway beyond the idling traffic eyes behind
windshields a few people coming out of stores buildings
evaporated sky obliterated suddenly pierced by her face her face
inside his face and hears himself reply "Still here!" her dark lips
open like a chalice

Louise

he was explaining why Berryman was such a fervent poet his ear
    especially his full weird ear unbelievable
he flailed his arms he wept he described virtues of the verse unclear
    in the dream but clear in the way felt detail is when it occurs too
    fast to remember
he was sitting on stone steps behind a castle
he was with a woman who seemed enthralled by the talk
he was in Berryman's mood before the leap from a bridge much
    younger than he was
he was able to quote from any book instantaneously wept many
    times while he recited lines thousands printed black on white
    sticks stacked in a colossal box jumbled pointing up toward
he crying in her arms about an obscure grief she held him what was
    this who was this with him Louise the name Louise sung by
    sheer air in a shattering abstract tone but he still didn't know
    "know" wove itself into the voice then Rembrandt in 1660
    wearing a square tan cap white band on bottom edge looks out at
    us as always in the self-portraits unashamed baffled resigned to
    a sorrow whose justice he cannot accept the mouth hoping to
    speak torso of brownish cloth scarcely painted lower part of the
    face dark eyes dark cheeks lighter then the brow and cap front
    bright above ruby nose all ringed by a night of paint the thick
    band folded taut across forehead one crease wild star-white light

Dream

he sought their beauty like a hunting dog straining for scent the
    sweet pale lips the anything dreaming this last dream of recovery
    sainted acceptance
he was dancing in a hi-fi festival everyone was dancing drinking
    suddenly humping from behind someone in white she had a
    second body dressed in black
he couldn't tell which one he was having until both came at the
    same time then ran into their house on the edge of the crowd
    stood in the lighted windows undressed to underwear the whole
    family facing him hand in hand dancing a jig smiling celebrating
    lust life the flesh and blood mortal moment in their tiny house
    then shift to vivid apartment under construction next to his in an
    old elegant building
he saw lavish renovations through the open door room upon room of
    glass soft furniture kitchenware the floor still dull unfinished
    wood but the landlord steps out into the hall claims he owes him
    fifty bucks for what I forget and I say Go fuck yourself the wild
    music fading dancers and dance one unheard invisible
he woke wondering what it could mean such deep happiness such
    concrete flimsy imagery that lives only inside a head whose
    lease on the real was impossible to whistle

Thread

he found spool after spool in his mother's sewing stand after her
    death antique lacquered Chinese hand-painted birds pale yellow
    grasses decorating it
he thought almost every color must be there
he found scissors needles slipped everywhere into the blue plush
    cushion tacked under the lid
he unearthed a silver thimble tape measure hunks of cloth a plastic
    box of buttons pins in a red cotton cushion shaped like a tomato
he found snippets of thread rolled into pellets saved for some obscure
    reason in a small brown paper bag
he knew she loved to sew but had never watched her do it never seen
    her fix a rip or put on a button had never been given the
    privilege of the sight of her unaware of him when he visited no
    that would be impossible he had to be seen she had to know
    where he was what he was doing she had to listen to his hands
    touch things be able to respond to his words or not by adopting
    one of her deliberately mystifying silences she had to be sure he
    didn't leave a crumb behind or shift a glass out of its place she
    must impart her sense of the ominous teeth tongue wetting
    twirling the tip of a thread then guiding it through the eye of the
    bright needle

Hooks

he sits facing him the same theme the same analytic toil
he doesn't want to face this but wants to
he has to understand this fears his fears to be free
he hears words like birds trying to talk human
he no he does hear the words in the room as real words
he understands interprets questions answers thinks
he sits in the leather chair provided across from him
he was a child and is again and is not definitely not but his pain is a
    broken toy
he brings in words like need disappoint empower symbiosis the last
    the crucial one
he uses words in the room like a tweezers or pickax
he cannot break through this inchworm process of
he refuses to decide what the process is
he can't stop it wants to stop it can't live though he lives
he knows the imaginary life breeds self-consciousness
he wants each session to chip off another gram of dread
he knows his sense of a dead fetus clarifies the root of his incurable
    his crippled brand of love
he must go back again over the same theme that tells itself in words
    in memories in life in silence again again
he asks why again his problem remains intractable unsolved
he hammers at himself with his mother's for God's sake find new
    names for this with Her Introjected Mind
he's like a man focusing the right eyepiece on binoculars left right
    left until the field's clear nothing in the field his chest bursts with
    futile desire

they are facing each other silent which often happens the therapist
stops looking out the window turns reports "I had this patient in
the hospital who lived with his mother until he was forty, when
he met a woman he wanted to marry. On the day he moved out,
she was waiting in the vestibule–punched him in the face, bit his
neck. One session he told me he dreamed his mother naked. Her
breasts were shaped like hooks."

Death

he got a call from an ex-friend just in from Paris for his daughter's
    wedding reminded him today he's sixty! heard him scream with
    fear-joy joy-disbelief rattle his throat in funny anguish ask if he
    remembered he sent a gift from Paris twenty years back wallet
    with photo in it of an old man getting blown
he was amazed by this man's compassion to remember such a great
    thing so kind so tinged with grief's affection
he thought an old man getting blown well-blown now that's really
    something don't you think it was as if his muse were whispering
    some key to the universe O blown O taken in like that in the wet
    compliment of tongue of lips mouth sensitive to so sensitive a
    place place of himself one might say
he thanked his ex-friend in his mind after they hung up it was just
    like him to find a splinter of time sharp with pleasure to inspire
    him an old man getting a blowjob well well well whispered his
    muse because she seemed to like repeating it so much he
    thought he'd hire her permanently
he sat alone for awhile after the call not in love to figure out where
    that damned wallet and snapshot went dug through several
    drawers tried to resurrect what where sifted through old boxes
    madly
he knew surely belief in God was extraneous under such
    circumstances as these provided by his deep dear ex-friend then
    this entered his mind or was it his muse once more at his ear
    teaching him truth how poignant dumb names are why if we die
    do we need them Steve Bill Jeff Michael Chris Tom Len Sidney

Dust

he thought a god might save whatever was left of his life it could be a
  bleak idea image sketched in the air trace of some myth some
  clump of darkness shabby poisonously real
he thought the god could be one of those Picasso men drawn to look
  like gods penis balls obvious fluid lines relaxed girl in his arms
  giving herself
he imagined it above him below him all the more potent because
  invisible all empty air all nothing a hand or eye can grasp
he would close his eyes dredge up dream images try combinations
  meanings interpreted unsought visions versions of self-dust self-
  loss until No-self image interfered
he manipulated himself to sit spine straight letting mind be mind no
  hands no feet a mere small bundle breathing
he woke often at three in the dark seeking the walls seeking the floor
  seeking questionless answers lay there two bodies breathing
he told fragmentary stories that summed up battles between the I
  and the above-I not lost not won except psyche remained psyche
  even moreso
he deliberated psyche's sphynxlike voiceless being its ability to see
  hear speak and breathe its unborn infinite root in chaos cosmos
  which word fits? which doesn't? he at times saw himself as a
  stick beating a stick a pathetic clacking to flush out angels
he studied angels in paintings too plump rosy inane babies of false
  peace false wakefulness
he once saw shoelaces glow *as is* as real shoelaces mystically limited
  perfected plastic tip texture length hue immediate signs of
  immanence
he concocted gods by aching for begging for praying for "To pile like
  Thunder to its close Then crumble grand away While Everything
  created hid This—would be Poetry—Or Love—the two coeval
  come—We both and neither prove—Experience either and
  consume—For None see God and live—"

he knew dust had been given to him in the shape of his own body
   would be blown away blown far away signed a letter "until our
   dusts reach Venus" to prove friendship
he knew he had been given to the world its earth its air its sky been
   given to what must have its dust back dust again and would soon

Windows

he turned the page to a shot of three tall Yonkers factory windows
   gorged with fire two firemen backs toward him climbing a white
   truck ladder angled at the building's corner blank space beyond
he couldn't get clear the force these windows filled with fire had on
   his mind like a layer of consciousness that's so old deep nothing
   can reach it though it still exists
he saw the men outside approaching the blaze frozen in the news
   photo one with an air bottle on his back explorers willing to die
   for knowledge
he also realized the flame seemed to roil upward transcending the
   dead time in a still shot seemed roaringly livid with itself a
   formless bestial thing contained only by the windows' shape as it
   reached out
he even might have dreamt the transfiguration of Mankind because
   of it one night recently though this morning it was there on his
   desk an ordinary newspaper image torn from the *New York
   Times*
he counted every brick every diagonal brace on the ladder then
   stared left into the nothing of the sky over the fighters' heads
   those demi-gods in afflicted postures leaning away from the heat
   preparing to enter
he noticed when he focused properly two dark posts inside the frame
   dividing the windows their top halves eaten away effigies with
   heads swirled to a point by fire the huge square three-part
   window dissolving bitten away at the edges

Sky

he couldn't have predicted it would defile sleep image after same
    image when he stood in the big green field
he heard the sky crack like a heated platter
he stood there too terrified to look up
he thought a real field? field in a dream?
he heard it repeat until it became one din changed into his face
    pointed up at the sky then thundered starting on the right
    incrementally each equal portion whining like a long nail pried
    from a board
which proved *psyche* was the first god
which defined the silence filling his mouth
which took him to the edge of his dream
which would not let him wake until it was law
which promised crucifixion when he woke
which etched a black breach straight all the way across the sky the
    same inside him across the top of his skull
is that where the sky ends?
what's on the other side?

Cry

he faced the imperious tall Queen in a tortoiseshell neckbrace
shoulders to chin

he was half-hypnotized by her force her near-death freedom to
demand anything to risk herself viciously hired by the gods to
execute anyone for anything

he saw her lean on her long wolf-headed cane carved out of orange
wood flecked with silver

he stared at her hand breast-high squatting on the head like a
mammoth spider

he recognized his mother's spike-like face its mien like an oath of
silence rebuking him brutal domineering the time she dug her
nails into his neck or screamed he should die

he saw darkness smudged under her eyes some wraith was leading
her to a room a bed where she would die he stood up facing her
stared into her eyes heard her command he obeyed heard one of
those selves we have that can wait years to speak say "I won't
take care of you tomorrow"

she must be in that room now that bed that sacrosanct threshold
where she'll never die no death in the mind without identity
mind outside the mind

he thought each thing we see is a surface whose other side has no
identity like the side of a wall we don't see

he knew the dream was over when he decided to let her die

he was lying in bed counting slats on a window shade watching the
light get whiter thinking bones how strange to watch his mother
die in a hospital bed three years ago see her again engrossed by
the disease so out of it all she could do was grope blindly cry to
be lifted out of bed acquitted bones desperate for the white
plastic potty every other minute

Riding

he passed huge scraps of bark the size of his arm curled on the
    pavement where he rode
he hauled through heaps of smaller pieces musty wafts of scent
    clutching his throat saw signs everywhere leaves crumbled areas
    of leaves gone brown over his head the sycamore's ungainly
    blotchy trunk old limbs lopped off always guarding the road
    unbeautiful the sweet mild transitives of death blown
    everywhere
he was in a dream again no grim abrasive soul no hope no-no
    yearning no regret pushed each foot forward down as always
    strapped onto the pedals
he watched the river's glittering white skin for a mile ahead nothing
    of its look amazed him it merely squirmed a little on his left
he followed it
he rushed past the usual lovers stretched out touching some face to
    face some angled staring up leaning on their sides kids wobbly
    on skates joggers amateurs pros
he looked right to Remington's *Cowboy* rearing up on its hillside
    rock and left to the words called *Sleeping Woman* glazed on the
    stone retaining wall "How can you know what it means to be
    here" it begins
he could see a scrim of thin mist drawn across the horizon of
    treetops far downriver
he could locate campers by the chocks of bloody char gusting from
    barbecues
he spotted rivulets of transparent silver flattened across cliffs spill
    down disappear
he observed tame geese nibbling grass on either side of the bike path
    refuse to notice him or move no matter how hard he pounded
    past

he cruised in some primitive immortal realm of being alive between one place and another poised momentarily in a long cave of sanity where past and future have not yet touched the finite before they fuse forever in the here now he didn't even need to mock it as theory it was real this great good room of life this blessed gift of faith in well it didn't really matter

Cloak

he saw sweetness darkness heard syllables detached from words
   seeking words
he experienced the sanctum of remorse where All or One is nothing
   but verbs no subjects objects
he saw the room where madness sits that can't compromise
he vanished down bronze-rimmed stairs into the holy earth
he was in a room somewhere talking to his mother who was
   distraught about her mother who was lost somewhere near the
   ocean out of her mind must be helped aura of panic and calm
   must find her then everything would be
he stood in the office of theory more accurately space where infinite
   and finite endow even a rat or a coffee cup with sacred luminous
   tones
he did not decide that day to walk into the noon service of the Baptist
   Church on 17th but was compelled each step the edge of the last
   seated behind the sobbing black woman shabby Christ nailed up
   in tarnished gold scattered worshipers ill-dressed minister
   talking not preaching about the this the that the religion his face
   a hopeless void until a sentence tore his heart out "The One who
   accepts you as you are" and "beside you . . . difficult to see . . .
   must try"
he wanted the dream of mothers to explain once and for all mothers
   seeking mothers the chain of life phrases crumbling as he woke
   and fell back to sleep into it hearing it losing it
he needed a different mind to live if he was supposed to understand
   survive
he could feel the darkness lift itself onto its own shoulders bleak
   sickening cloak or was it the female singer in the church doing a
   hymn

he knew the physical version of the metaphysical in this because or
    was it the mythical its ghosts its ontic where? why? its feral
    belief that if only the mother could be seen again touched again
    all would be cured even death though the opposite's true
he was defeated by it because he knew no version of it worked
    settled things gave meanings he lacked to say it
he had finally stood on the threshold of the *I* at least glimpsed its
    false promise of release: the side where only things exist they do
    and we do but death doesn't matter this was the background
    reality of the dream the universal core ". . . who accepts you as
    you are"
he knelt he heard "Where's my mother?" a child's shrill singsong
    from his mother's lips on her deathbed
he could feel the darkness resurrecting us as itself bare black
    darkness instead of us
you sometimes find in books and museums certain primitive shards
    facsimiles of proofs of a rawness the pure idiotic marrow of the
    sky harvested shapeless draped on absent shoulders

Mortality

he was on the phone sitting in the kitchen talking to one friend then
 another both mentioned Time with a capital T one said "It drives
 me crazy" the other "Ignore it, we're as immortal as the
 moment"
he sat there after the calls looked at things bare lily stems ivy weeds
 a row of black porcelain bowls made by Toshiko books knives
 cups glasses fruit his own big feet in biking shoes ready to ride
he was doing all the usual shit to avoid the ride before the ride
he was brooding as usual about what could not be changed
he was thinking about his friend's daughter's wedding that night
he was wondering which shirt he'd wear probably the deep blue
 French cuffs plain collar
he had a list for after the ride cigars pick up shirts yogurt cash
he felt dread seep from belly to chest fill his chest spread then
 dissolve watched degrees of light tried to see only light light
 without leaves or any object it revealed impossible that task of
 concentration that gate of revelation that escape from death that
 flight into flesh's destiny
he remembered another call yesterday a new friend's twenty-year-
 old daughter had died in a car wreck the woman said when she
 walked down the street now she sought cigarette butts if her
 daughter could not see beautiful things she could not bear to
 either she wanted only butts When I wake each day she said
 there's a spotlight on me
he ached with silence sitting there dressed for his ride
he typed out Henry James's last dictation undated in coma "across
 the border all the pieces Individual souls, great . . . [word lost] on
 which great perfections are If one does . . . in the fulfillment with
 the neat and pure and perfect—to the success or has he or she
 moves through life, following admiration unfailing [word lost] in
 the highway—Problems are very sordid"

Illinois Poetry Series

Laurence Lieberman, Editor

History Is Your Own Heartbeat
Michael S. Harper (1971)

The Foreclosure
Richard Emil Braun (1972)

The Scrawny Sonnets and Other
Narratives
Robert Bagg (1973)

The Creation Frame
Phyllis Thompson (1973)

To All Appearances: Poems New
and Selected
Josephine Miles (1974)

The Black Hawk Songs
Michael Borich (1975)

Nightmare Begins Responsibility
Michael S. Harper (1975)

The Wichita Poems
Michael Van Walleghen (1975)

Images of Kin: New and Selected
Poems
Michael S. Harper (1977)

Poems of the Two Worlds
Frederick Morgan (1977)

Cumberland Station
Dave Smith (1977)

Tracking
Virginia R. Terris (1977)

Riversongs
Michael Anania (1978)

On Earth as It Is
Dan Masterson (1978)

Coming to Terms
Josephine Miles (1979)

Death Mother and Other Poems
Frederick Morgan (1979)

Goshawk, Antelope
Dave Smith (1979)

Local Men
James Whitehead (1979)

Searching the Drowned Man
Sydney Lea (1980)

With Akhmatova at the Black Gates
Stephen Berg (1981)

Dream Flights
Dave Smith (1981)

More Trouble with the Obvious
Michael Van Walleghen (1981)

The American Book of the Dead
Jim Barnes (1982)

The Floating Candles
Sydney Lea (1982)

Northbook
Frederick Morgan (1982)

Collected Poems, 1930–83
Josephine Miles (1983; reissue, 1999)

The River Painter
Emily Grosholz (1984)

Healing Song for the Inner Ear
Michael S. Harper (1984)

The Passion of the Right-Angled Man
T. R. Hummer (1984)

Dear John, Dear Coltrane
Michael S. Harper (1985)

Poems from the Sangamon
John Knoepfle (1985)

In It
Stephen Berg (1986)

The Ghosts of Who We Were
Phyllis Thompson (1986)

Moon in a Mason Jar
Robert Wrigley (1986)

Lower-Class Heresy
T. R. Hummer (1987)

Poems: New and Selected
Frederick Morgan (1987)

Furnace Harbor: A Rhapsody of the North Country
Philip D. Church (1988)

Bad Girl, with Hawk
Nance Van Winckel (1988)

Blue Tango
Michael Van Walleghen (1989)

Eden
Dennis Schmitz (1989)

Waiting for Poppa at the Smithtown Diner
Peter Serchuk (1990)

Great Blue
Brendan Galvin (1990)

What My Father Believed
Robert Wrigley (1991)

Something Grazes Our Hair
S. J. Marks (1991)

Walking the Blind Dog
G. E. Murray (1992)

The Sawdust War
Jim Barnes (1992)

The God of Indeterminacy
Sandra McPherson (1993)

Off-Season at the Edge of the World
Debora Greger (1994)

Counting the Black Angels
Len Roberts (1994)

Oblivion
Stephen Berg (1995)

To Us, All Flowers Are Roses
Lorna Goodison (1995)

Honorable Amendments
Michael S. Harper (1995)

Points of Departure
Miller Williams (1995)

Dance Script with Electric Ballerina
Alice Fulton (reissue, 1996)

To the Bone: New and Selected Poems
Sydney Lea (1996)

Floating on Solitude
Dave Smith (3-volume reissue, 1996)

Bruised Paradise
Kevin Stein (1996)

Walt Whitman Bathing
David Wagoner (1996)

Rough Cut
Thomas Swiss (1997)

Paris
Jim Barnes (1997)

The Ways We Touch
Miller Williams (1997)

The Rooster Mask
Henry Hart (1998)

The Trouble-Making Finch
Len Roberts (1998)

Grazing
Ira Sadoff (1998)

Turn Thanks
Lorna Goodison (1999)

Traveling Light: Collected and
New Poems
David Wagoner (1999)

Some Jazz a While: Collected Poems
Miller Williams (1999)

The Iron City
John Bensko (2000)

Songlines in Michaeltree: New and
Collected Poems
Michael S. Harper (2000)

Pursuit of a Wound
Sydney Lea (2000)

The Pebble: Old and New Poems
Mairi MacInnes (2000)

Chance Ransom
Kevin Stein (2000)

House of Poured-Out Waters
Jane Mead (2001)

The Silent Singer: New and Selected
Poems
Len Roberts (2001)

The Salt Hour
J. P. White (2001)

Guide to the Blue Tongue
Virgil Suárez (2002)

The House of Song
David Wagoner (2002)

X =
Stephen Berg (2002)

National Poetry Series

Eroding Witness
Nathaniel Mackey (1985)
Selected by Michael S. Harper

Palladium
Alice Fulton (1986)
Selected by Mark Strand

Cities in Motion
Sylvia Moss (1987)
Selected by Derek Walcott

The Hand of God and a Few
Bright Flowers
William Olsen (1988)
Selected by David Wagoner

The Great Bird of Love
Paul Zimmer (1989)
Selected by William Stafford

Stubborn
Roland Flint (1990)
Selected by Dave Smith

The Surface
Laura Mullen (1991)
Selected by C. K. Williams

The Dig
Lynn Emanuel (1992)
Selected by Gerald Stern

My Alexandria
Mark Doty (1993)
Selected by Philip Levine

The High Road to Taos
Martin Edmunds (1994)
Selected by Donald Hall

Theater of Animals
Samn Stockwell (1995)
Selected by Louise Glück

The Broken World
Marcus Cafagña (1996)
Selected by Yusef Komunyakaa

Nine Skies
A. V. Christie (1997)
Selected by Sandra McPherson

Lost Wax
Heather Ramsdell (1998)
Selected by James Tate

So Often the Pitcher Goes to Water
until It Breaks
Rigoberto González (1999)
Selected by Ai

Renunciation
Corey Marks (2000)
Selected by Philip Levine

Manderley
Rebecca Wolff (2001)
Selected by Robert Pinsky

Theory of Devolution
David Groff (2002)
Selected by Mark Doty

Other Poetry Volumes

Local Men and *Domains*
James Whitehead (1987)

Her Soul beneath the Bone:
Women's Poetry on Breast Cancer
Edited by Leatrice Lifshitz (1988)

Days from a Dream Almanac
Dennis Tedlock (1990)

Working Classics: Poems on
Industrial Life
*Edited by Peter Oresick and
Nicholas Coles* (1990)

Hummers, Knucklers, and Slow
Curves: Contemporary Baseball
Poems
Edited by Don Johnson (1991)

The Double Reckoning of
Christopher Columbus
Barbara Helfgott Hyett (1992)

Selected Poems
Jean Garrigue (1992)

New and Selected Poems, 1962–92
Laurence Lieberman (1993)

The Dig and *Hotel Fiesta*
Lynn Emanuel (1994)

For a Living: The Poetry of Work
*Edited by Nicholas Coles and
Peter Oresick* (1995)

The Tracks We Leave: Poems on
Endangered Wildlife of North
America
Barbara Helfgott Hyett (1996)

Peasants Wake for Fellini's
Casanova and Other Poems
*Andrea Zanzotto; edited and
translated by John P. Welle and Ruth
Feldman; drawings by Federico
Fellini and Augusto Murer* (1997)

Moon in a Mason Jar and *What My
Father Believed*
Robert Wrigley (1997)

The Wild Card: Selected Poems,
Early and Late
*Karl Shapiro; edited by Stanley
Kunitz and David Ignatow* (1998)

Turtle, Swan and *Bethlehem in
Broad Daylight*
Mark Doty (2000)

Illinois Voices: An Anthology of
Twentieth-Century Poetry
*Edited by Kevin Stein and
G. E. Murray* (2001)

On a Wing of the Sun
Jim Barnes (3-volume reissue, 2001)

Poems
*William Carlos Williams;
introduction by Virginia M. Wright-
Peterson* (2002)

The University of Illinois Press
is a founding member of the
Association of American University Presses.

Composed in 9.5 /14 Walbaum Book
with Lubalin Graph display
by Celia Shapland
for the University of Illinois Press
Designed by Copenhaver Cumpston
Manufactured by Thomson-Shore, Inc.

University of Illinois Press
1325 South Oak Street
Champaign, IL 61820-6903
www.press.uillinois.edu